Shortcuts to

keeping
your cool

Gael Lindenfield

To Polly (Gibson) Jones

In love and admiration for the way you persisted in your struggle to deal constructively with your feelings in the face of so many frustrations.

Acknowledgements for the
Shortcuts Series

First, thanks again to all the people who have so openly shared their struggles with me. I hope that you will be pleased that the wisdom I gained from your difficult experiences has been constructively channelled into these Shortcut strategies.

Secondly, many special thanks to Jo Kyle who has done such a magnificent job with the editing of these books. Working with Jo in cyberspace has opened my eyes up to the amazing potential of electronic relationships. I have learned to trust and respect the judgement of someone simply through the exchange of written words. (A good lesson for a writer!)

Thirdly, the Thorsons team has been as patient, supportive and willing to experiment as ever. A big thank you to each and every one of you.

Fourthly, *muchas gracias a mis amigos en* La Puebla de Los Infantes who fed and entertained me so often while I was in Spain writing much of this series. You were an inspiration as well as a support.

Finally, once again my husband Stuart's contribution must be acknowledged. The title of this series was his idea. As ever, I am also grateful to him for giving over so much of his precious free time to edit my dyslexic manuscripts before they leave the privacy of our home.

Other titles in the series:

Contents

Introduction to the
Shortcuts Series

At this moment in your life, reading a book is probably one of the last things you feel like doing. If so, you are exactly the kind of reader I had in mind when I designed this Shortcuts series!

I have struggled with enough personal problems myself to know that when you are in the throes of them, the thought of wading through any book is daunting. You just haven't got the concentration or the motivation. When I am in this situation, all I long for is for someone to tell me what to do – or, even better, relieve me of my hurt or worry by taking it away from me!

So I would like you to think of these Shortcuts guides not so much as books but as supportive *tools*. I do not intend them to be like an absorbing 'read' to take to the sofa or bath and get 'lost' in. On the contrary, they are designed as 'ready-made' strategies to help kick you into action – and to keep you moving over a period of one to two months – at least! (Isn't 'the getting going' always the hardest part of solving any problem? This is when I have found that even the most competent and self-reliant people can benefit from support.)

But it is also important that when we do get started, we begin in a *constructive* way. A common mistake is to *do* the first thing that comes into our mind. This can make us feel better because we *feel* more in control. But this 'hit and miss' approach often gets us going on a very much longer and rockier road than we need have taken. In contrast, these Shortcut strategies will guide you along a route that has been meticulously planned. They are derived from years of experimentation and studying other people's tried and tested paths.

The first characteristic of each book that you may notice (and perhaps find initially frustrating) is that they all start with some preparation work. This is because, in my experience, diving headlong into the heart of the problem often proves to be the shortcut to failure!

After you have prepared yourself, the strategy moves along in a series of small steps, each with its own section. Although sometimes these steps will overlap, most of the time you should find that one naturally follows on from the other. At the end of each, you will find a list of tips called 'Action time!'. Some of the suggestions and exercises in this section may work better for you than others. But I am confident that in the process of trying them, you are much more likely to find out what *will* help than if you did nothing at all! So I hope you will find them of use one way or another.

Throughout the book you will also find some quotes and key 'messages' (highlighted in bold type). I hope you will find these useful should you just want to dip into the book and gain some quick support and guidance at times when the going feels tough.

Finally, I would like you to always bear in mind that in the personal development field there are no prizes for being first to the winning post. But there are, however, plenty of rewards to be had from the *effective* learning of problem-solving skills. So if you proceed through these Shortcuts books at a pace which feels **comfortably challenging**, you will have

learned an invaluable skill that could save you time
and energy for the rest of your life.

Enjoy the journey! (Yes, problem solving *can* be
highly pleasurable!)

Introduction

Anger is dangerous.

But *not* being angry can be highly dangerous too.

These are the two crucial messages that you will find underlying this whole Shortcut strategy.

Our objective is not anger abstinence. Indeed, this Shortcut strategy is a programme designed for people of passion. It's for people who *value* their right to anger when they are faced with injustice, abuse or threat – indeed, to such an extent that they are willing to do some tough self-control work in order to keep it.

Have you been frightened off yet? I doubt it. People who lose their cool are rarely quickly intimidated!

This is one of your great qualities. But perhaps you have already lost sight of it, along with many other qualities you must possess.

Being someone with temper problems means that you will be frequently faced with the less virtuous sides of you. Perhaps you have picked up this book because you have already been behaving in ways which you freely acknowledge are wrong. You are probably very similar to the many people with whom I have worked on anger management. They are not essentially 'bad' people but they are very aware that when they are in a temper they do (or know they could) behave in ways which they themselves hate and which are dangerous for both them and others. For example, they may have:

- shouted at (or even hit) an innocent child and are now mortified to see the child stand in fear of them
- ranted at a powerless front-desk person and reduced them to tears so they were unable to continue working
- hurt someone they loved by saying things about them that were patently exaggerated or untrue

It took, however, a great deal of **humility** and **courage** for these people to face these less attractive aspects of themselves. And I guess that it also probably took a fair amount of these exact same personal qualities for you to take even a tentative glance at this introduction. When such qualities are combined with an ability to feel deep anger and express it in a safe and constructive way, I believe you have the recipe for a potential hero. (With the added advantage of being a hero who still lives to tell the tale!)

How you use your 'heroic' power will, of course, be up to you. For example, you could use it to:

- stand up for your own right to be heard within your family
- champion the needs of the office underdogs
- stand up to your child's teacher when you disagree with her or his approach
- complain vociferously and persistently when you meet bad service

or even,

- revolutionize your country by ensuring your politicians practise what they preach
- radically change the world by 'fighting' to give peace a chance

And all this without once losing your cool!

An impossible goal? Well, I'll admit there might be a chance of an occasional slip en route. But, generally speaking, I do believe that you can have your anger cake and eat it. And once you do, you can become a very powerful agent for effecting change without hurting others with uncontrolled aggression or yourself with tension-producing repression. This strategy is not just a figment of my fertile imagination – its plan and suggestions are drawn from many years of practical experience of anger management. (Firstly, with my own temper, and subsequently with courageous clients.)

What is the

Shortcut Strategy?

As you will see, our Shortcut strategy for keeping your cool is divided into four stages:

STAGE 1:   **Preparing Yourself**

STAGE 2:   **Empowering Yourself**

STAGE 3:   **Retraining Your Auto-Responses**

STAGE 4:   **Staying Cool – Forever!**

Each of these stages contains a number of steps. As you might expect, some stages require more time and work than others. For instance, Stage 3 is the heart of the matter so it contains many more steps than the others. But don't be tempted to rush headlong into this stage for some quick answers. The other three are equally important, even if they are shorter or not so directly relevant to your current concerns. I assure you that these are the ones that will ensure that your work in Stage 3 is not wasted. (You will understand why as you work your way through them.)

As I suggested in the general introduction to this Shortcuts series, this self-help strategy normally takes up to two months to complete. But that is on the understanding that you will devote at least two hours per week to doing the exercises and practice that I suggest. If it takes longer, don't despair. For a whole variety of complex reasons, some people's emotional habits take longer to crack than others'. (And there is no shame in being different from the crowd, is there?)

Have patience with yourself en route! At times you may find the strategy tough going, but overall it should prove to be enlightening and quickly rewarding.

Stage One

preparing yourself

This stage is an important preparatory one. It is about increasing your understanding of both yourself and your anger response. The extra wisdom you will gain from spending time on the following exercises will pay immense dividends, as it will help motivate you by making sense of the work you will be doing later. The first step will also ensure that you don't short-change yourself by not setting aside enough time to work on this strategy.

STEP 1

Get motivated to protect some quality time

Of course you are in a hurry to get a handle on your temper. (And no doubt you are not the only one who would like you to get your anger act together with great speed!) But this isn't going to happen unless you are prepared to do what I have suggested in the Introduction. You *must* set aside some quality time to work on this strategy. The very minimum amount needed would be two hours per week over the next one to two months.

Maybe at this very moment you do feel very determined to change. It is likely that something major, or someone important, has 'driven' you to read this book. You could even be living under the shadow of an ultimatum. This is a common reason for taking the uncomfortable plunge into anger management. And it's not a bad reason. It shows that you care about something or someone. It also indicates that there is a fair degree of pain or fear in your life. Both will undoubtedly give you a good 'kick-start', but they are unlikely to be enough to keep you to task should the going get tough or tedious.

To stay committed to this strategy, **you** *also* **need to be positively motivated by the convincing prospect of long-lasting pleasure for YOU.** That's the kind of psychological driving force that separates the winners from the losers on this kind of playing field.

Time is obviously a highly precious commodity to someone with a temperament like yours. That's one of the reasons why you lose your cool so readily. Isn't it true that you haven't much patience with time-wasters? Aren't you less inclined than some others to wait around for people to explain themselves (again!) or for the long-term solutions to fix the messes that you think require immediate attention.

And, once again, that's no bad thing. (In moderation, of course!) But being someone who is always in a hurry means that you will find it extra difficult to reserve quality time to work on this strategy. So, in order to do this, you will need to take extra care to keep your motivation positively boosted.

> **A vision of the rewards that you will receive for keeping your cool is even more motivating than the fear of what will happen if you don't.**

Action time!

- **Write down the tangible long-term pleasures (as opposed to the absence of punishment) that you will gain from taking control of your temper.** You can add to this list over the next few weeks as more rewards come to mind. Try to bring each example more alive in your mind by making it as positive and specific as possible:

  Here are some examples:

  'I'll have a great quality one-to-one relationship with ___' (rather than, *'I'll stop falling out with everyone'*)
  'I will stand a good chance of becoming a ___ at work' (instead of, *'I won't lose my job'*)
  'I'll have more energy so I will be able to ___' (rather than, *'I won't die of an early heart attack'*)

- **Take yourself into a state of deep relaxation.** (Soaking in a warm aromatic bath with relaxing music is an excellent way to achieve this, but you could also try the exercise on pages 96-99) Then, when you are deeply relaxed, close your eyes and form a picture of yourself in your mind's eye appearing cool, calm and collected. Study this mental image in detail. Look at your relaxed facial expression and posture and *feel* the sense of confidence with which this image resonates. Notice how much pleasure this feeling is giving you.

Now, with your eyes still closed, imagine that you are watching a mental movie of this calm, confident you *enjoying* life in five years time. (You will be enjoying most if not all the rewarding pleasures you listed above.) Once again, make a conscious effort to *feel* the pleasure that these imagined scenes bring to mind.

Repeat this exercise frequently over the next few months, especially at times when your motivation needs an extra boost.

Emotions have their own agenda and timetable, but our rushed lives give them no space, no airtime – and so they go underground ... we typically become aware of emotions only when they build up and boil over.

DANIEL GOLEMAN

STEP 2

Increase your knowledge of how anger works

Although I have never had any conscious desire to become a wild animal trainer, perhaps I could have become one. My approach to taming anger appears to have many similarities! I believe it is very important to develop some understanding of the nature of the 'beast' before learning the art of training it. When we understand how anger works, we immediately feel less overawed by it.

But the analogy with wild beast taming has its limits. There is a serious price to pay for getting more wised-up about anger. It is called responsibility! Once we understand how the anger response works, unfortunately there are no more excuses and there is no more 'buck-passing'. (I'm not sure animal training carries this kind of burden, but I would be interested to know if it does!)

The pay off for believing that anger is a mysterious force within us is that it reduces the guilt that goes with managing it badly. We feel freer to offload the responsibility for coping with the consequences of our own behaviour. We may even pass the buck in the victim's direction!

Do any of these examples ring bells with you?

'I know I have been tetchy all day – don't take it so personally. Don't you ever get out of the wrong side of the bed sometimes?'
(A supervisor 'explaining' why she had just unfairly snapped at someone in her team)

'I heard myself swearing and it felt as though I was listening to someone else. But I couldn't stop myself. It was awful.'
(A manager who 'lost it' in an important meeting at work)

'Of course I didn't mean it – I was just angry. You shouldn't be so sensitive – lighten up. I know I am a bit fiery at times, but that's just the way I am – I can't help being me.'
(A young woman talking to her boyfriend after a fall out between them)

*'I didn't mean to hit him. I don't know how it happened –
I just lost it. It was when he gave me that insolent look.'*
(A loving mother in a parenting group talking about
hitting her son)

*'She'd been nagging me all evening and I was tired – I
had had enough. It had been a terrible day at work.
Then she brushed past me saying she was off to stay
with her sister – then all I can remember is going cold
and grabbing hold of her.'*
(A man talking about hurting his girlfriend)

Just writing the above has brought back many
reminders of times when I used to habitually lay the
blame for my own temper outbursts on either my
Irish genes, my PMT or other people's irritating
habits. When I find myself doing this now, I stop my
'blame game' in its tracks by reminding myself of how
anger works. Doing this faces me with the uncomfortable truth about my responsibility (i.e. it is not
up to anyone else to find a way of putting up with
my moods and outbursts – and I don't deserve sympathy when I lose my cool!)

Do you take full responsibility for your own anger? If not, gaining a bit more understanding about how your anger response works might also help you to do so. You certainly don't need a degree in psychology or psychiatry to be able to keep your cool, but even a minimal understanding can make a great difference.

> **It is not up to anyone else to find a way of putting up with your moods and outbursts – and you don't deserve sympathy when you lose your cool!**

Action time!

- **Here is a summary of some of the relevant facts we have to date on the anger response.** They are the basis of the theory on which this strategy is based. Read them slowly and note your reaction to each.

The anger response ...
  - **is natural.** It is a self-protective physiological and emotional response which will automatically 'kick in' (in some form or other) whenever you are faced with threat, hurt, violation or frustration.
  - **is inevitable**. Unless your emotional system has been physiologically damaged or you isolate yourself on a dream desert island devoid of frustration and danger, you will feel anger.
  - **is designed to be temporary.** The biochemical changes that take place when you feel angry rev up your system into its 'top gear'. This gives you a 'shot' of increased strength and energy to cope with the situation. Prolonging this response will put a strain on your nervous system, organs and muscles. It will also distort your perception and reasoning.

Anger's Two Possible Emotional Journeys

NON-URGENT THREAT OR FRUSTRATION

IMMEDIATE DANGER!

| WISDOM WAY | JUNGLE SPEEDWAY |

Think through situation in cognitive centres of brain and choose or create an appropriate response

Select **stored blueprint response** from primitive emotional processing centre in the brain

Energize the body to act in a controlled and constructive manner to protect or problem-solve

Activate either **fight**, **flight** or **freeze** – physiologically fired response

- **can take one of two physiological journeys.**
In situations perceived to be emergencies, it
will be fast-tracked to a primitive emotional
centre in the brain, which will set off what is
commonly known as the 'fight/flight/freeze'
response. (I call this route **'The Jungle
Speedway'** – see the illustration opposite.)
This centre will select a response from a limited number of 'blueprints' derived from your
past experience of life – i.e. how you or others
have handled such situations before. (For
example, attack back with threatening verbal
abuse or fists (fight), leave the room or slam
the phone down and actively avoid confronting the issue again (flight), clam up and
say and do nothing, or suppress feelings and
act normally as though on 'auto-pilot' (freeze).)
In everyday situations, the anger response will
be sent to the more recently evolved thinking
centres of your brain. (I call this one **'The
Wisdom Way'** – see the illustration opposite.)
These centres can design a *tailor-made* and
possibly *new* response.
- **is individual.** No two people ever 'feel' exactly
the same way about an event. The quality and
quantity of your anger is coloured by a unique
blend of your genes, nurturing, culture,

environment, physical condition and existing emotional state.

- **is no respecter of reality.** If your brain mistakenly senses threat, hurt or violation, your emotional response will be the same as if this was really happening.
- **can be expressed safely and constructively.** Nobody or nothing can force you to lose your cool. If you choose to stay in control of your feelings, you can divert the energy generated by your anger into an assertive (or even a well-chosen passive) response.

Did you find it easy or hard to swallow and digest these key facts?

- **If they raised many questions for you, it may be advisable to swot up a little more on the subject.** So set aside some time soon to dip into (at the very least) another book on anger or the emotions. (For example, one of my earlier books, Managing Anger, or one of the other more general books on emotions suggested in the Recommended Reading list at the end of the book.) Alternatively, your doctor or some other knowledgeable person, such as a stress counsellor, may be able to clarify some of the points.

STEP 3

Train your own imaginary 'Anger Guide'

Now you understand how anger works in general, you need to know more specifically how it works for you. As I mentioned briefly in Step 2, our individual differences in relation to anger are caused by many factors, such as our genetically-inherited temperament, the culture which we were brought up in and the one we are living in now, and the significant role models we had in the past and the ones who are around for us in the present. This is why there can only be a few really effective general rules in the business of anger management. Instead, I suggest that instead of looking for simplistic general rules, you should think more along the lines of training your own imaginary 'Anger Guide'. (Catholics used to picturing in their mind their own Guardian Angel will know what I mean.)

So your job in this step is to provide your Anger Guide with a personalized map and set of instructions. **You will first need to make it super-aware of** *when* **and** *with whom* **you are most likely to lose your cool.** This will ensure that it will alert you the moment you meet an anger trigger. For example, mine has been instructed to get on guard when I:

- am rung by a 'cold-calling' salesperson
- encounter a 'false' smile
- hear a high-pitched whiny voice
- am battling with writer's block
- miss a deadline
- spot the slightest queue
- lose anything

These kinds of irritations may well be pure water off your back. My husband, for example, is more likely to lose his cool over matters which I often consider interesting challenges, and he is enraged by people for whom I frequently feel too sorry! (*Vive la différence!* What a boring world it would be without it.)

Secondly, your Anger Guide must also be informed about the way you are likely to express your feelings when your temper flares. Not everyone feels like throwing pots and pans at the wall, and not everyone lashes out with an acid tongue. But perhaps you could do either with certain people in certain situations, while at other times you 'flip' by just walking out, going silent or slamming down the phone.

Finally, your Anger Guide needs to be aware of how your *individual body* **will signal that your anger response is in action.** For example, some of us first feel tension in our back, while others can't keep their legs still or feel sick in their stomach. Our bodies react in a host of different ways depending on the unique physiology that we inherited and developed and, of course, the current state of our health.

So educating and training your Anger Guide is a very important task. Unless it has a very clear picture of your own special patterns, it cannot hope to prevent your anger from escalating towards the tantrum stage. The good news is that it doesn't require years of psychological analysis to be able to achieve a good-enough level of awareness. Normally a few hours of honest soul-searching and a subsequent dose of straight-talking from people who know you well does the trick.

> **You can train yourself to be
> one step ahead of your anger.**

Self-knowledge is the beginning of self-improvement.

SPANISH PROVERB

Action time!

- **Make some 'warning signal' notes for your Anger Guide using the following headings.** You may not be able to think of examples that relate to each of the headings at this moment, but perhaps you will be able to do so over the next few weeks.

  I am more inclined to lose my cool when:
  - *I am in these kinds of situations ... (at work/home /social life)*
  - *I am also experiencing these feelings or moods ...*
  - *It is this time of day/month/year ...*
  - *I hear these kinds of phrases or words ...*
  - *I see these kinds of facial expressions ...*
  - *I hear these kinds of tones of voice ...*
  - *I am with people who have these kinds of habits ...*
  - *I am with people who remind me of these people or these past events ...*
  - *I start eating and drinking more or less of these things ...*

- **Ask a few well-chosen friends and colleagues for some honest feedback about your anger patterns.** If they can't reply immediately, you

could show them the list above and then ask
them to closely observe you over the next month
or so and note when they think you are becoming frustrated or irritated. (They could well be
wrong, but often others can see our irritation
before we are aware of it, especially if we are a
very 'nice' person or behave in a habitually 'nice'
way. So don't dismiss observations if they do not
feel instantly right!)

- **Use the following list of potential 'symptoms'
  to help you identify the signs in your body
  which may indicate that you have started to
  become angry.** Note down your key ones.

  - **head** (for example, headaches, sinus pain,
    clenched jaw, fixed eyes)
  - **muscles** (for example, backache, tension in
    legs, shoulder or neck stiffness, clenched fists,
    finger tapping, more tightly crossed limbs,
    fidgeting)
  - **heart** (for example, heart beating faster)
  - **lungs** (for example, breathing more shallowly
    in upper chest, holding your breath, sighing,
    deep inhaling in order to increase voice
    volume)

   – **digestion** (for example, stomach cramps, frequent visits to the loo, wind, nausea, lack of appetite, stuffing yourself with food)

- **Add to your list any other pointers about your anger patterns that might be helpful to your Anger Guide.**

Stage Two

empowering
yourself

As I mentioned in the Introduction, losing our cool is not good for our self-confidence. It makes us lose trust in ourselves because we lose control and behave in ways which we later regret. So the following steps have been designed to make you feel better about yourself by boosting both your inner esteem and your physical energy. I can assure you that you will need good-enough levels of both to do the work in Stage 3!

Many of our problems with anger occur when we choose between having a relationship and having a self.

HARRIET GOLDHOR LERNER

STEP 4

Reinforce your self-esteem

Wounded pride is often the real trigger that causes us to lose our cool. Sometimes the 'hit' to our self-esteem comes directly in the form of blatant shaming. Perhaps you can recall situations where you 'lost it' when, for example, you were:

- criticized for a weakness (fairly or unfairly), especially in front of others
- had a mistake or failure publicly exposed
- had someone else's superior strengths or greater achievement 'thrown in your face'
- given 'second-class' treatment for being a minority or simply just for being too old or young, short or tall, fat or thin

Perhaps you may not have shown your anger directly at the time (we are often too shell-shocked to do so), but later you may have found yourself being unreasonably short-tempered with a friend or some stranger.

Sometimes the wound to our pride is less obvious. We may not even be aware with our conscious mind that we are feeling it. On reflection, I can see that travelling in rush hour – and being hustled and bustled like cattle into trains – knocks my self-respect. But when I arrive at my destination in an irritable state, I might explain my behaviour in terms of 'just a bad mood' or other people's 'infuriating habits'.

When the 'put-down' is more personal we may not face it because we don't want to believe it is happening. For example, after a recent promotion Jane started to be sidelined by her envious colleagues at lunchtimes. But instead of seeing their behaviour as an insult to her, she kept making excuses. For example, she would say to herself *'They must think I am too busy'/'They don't know how to handle the situation'/'Perhaps I am not handling it very well.'* (Even though she had been scrupulously fair and these friends were very socially competent.) She found herself becoming very irritable with her boyfriend in the evenings and nearly lost the relationship before she became aware that her wounded pride was the problem.

How sturdy is your self-esteem? Not sturdy enough, my experience of working with people who lose their cool would suggest. But then few of us can boast unwavering self-respect when we live in a world that is constantly confronting us with adverts and celebrities who are apparently perfect!

> **Reinforcing your self-esteem on a regular basis will render you much less vulnerable in the face of knocks to your pride, as well as bolstering your right to defend your self-respect in a constructive and assertive way.**

Action time!

- **Name three people who make you feel good about yourself when you are in their company.** Perhaps you know these people are like you and simply relish spending time with you. Or maybe they could be the kind who always inspire you and when you leave their company your head is buzzing with ideas of things you could do to stretch your potential. Now think of how you could increase the time you spend with these three people. Then, ask them if they would be prepared to do so. You should receive a positive self-esteem building response. If you don't, you will know that you have chosen the wrong person – so, after giving yourself a 'cheer-up' treat, find someone else fast.

- **With the help of your self-esteem building friends, work out how you can increase the number of experiences in your life that feed your sense of self-worth and pride and how you can decrease the ones that do the opposite.**

For example, you may decide to do more of the work which you excel at and speak honestly to your boss about the aspects of your job which you are struggling with. Or you could decide to give some time or money to a community project or offer to give one of your elderly neighbours a lift to the supermarket.

- **List a number of unfair criticisms that people could say about you which might rile you.** Beside each, write a short defence of yourself. You could also include the names of witnesses you could call on to add weight to your argument!

For example, sometimes people accuse me of trying to make money out of other people's suffering. In my defence, I would remind myself of the amount I earn compared to the amount I know I could earn in another area of work. I might also remind myself of the many clients whom I feel particularly proud of having helped.

- **List a number of your 'Achilles heels'** (i.e. the faults which you HATE people to remind you of). These could include fair criticisms which might make you fume, especially if given by the 'wrong' person at the wrong time in an inappropriate place. Beside each, write down how you could respond without losing your cool or inviting the critic to do so. (Turn to Step 13 for some examples of assertive language you could use.)

For example, it makes me fume when someone laughs at a spelling mistake I have made on a flip chart while I am trying to explain a difficult concept to someone else who is struggling to keep up in a workshop. In response, I could calmly explain that I suffer from dyslexia, apologize and carry straight on. Later, I could elicit some sympathy from an understanding colleague or my husband and I would probably give myself a compensatory treat!

STEP 5

Accept the devil within you

After a good dose of self-esteem building you should be in good shape to tackle this less pleasant step! It is designed to topple you off any high horses that you might be in the habit of riding. (Remember grandma recounting the proverb, 'People in glasshouses shouldn't throw stones'?!)

We often lose our cool when we feel consumed by an overwhelming fit of moral outrage. Occasionally your reaction might be entirely justifiable. Wickedness does exist and does deserve our anger. But on the whole I have found **people who lose their cool** *too* **frequently tend to be** *oversensitive* **about the 'sins' of others.**

The best antidote to an overabundance of self-right-
eousness is quite simply to eat a plate of humble pie.
The reason this works so well is that the sins that set
rapid light to our moral fire are the ones that we usually find hard to resist ourselves! Another trip into
my confessional box will help clarify this truth.

My blood has a tendency to boil the moment I am
inconvenienced by 'appallingly bad organization'
from someone who 'ought to know better'. This
could be a travel agent who has double booked our
hotel, a postal worker who cannot trace a parcel I
posted, or even my poor husband who omitted to
buy my hair conditioner because he mislaid the
shopping list!

Why do these understandable human errors offend
me *so* greatly? I am convinced it is because poor
organization is one of my own worst 'innate' faults. It
is a constant struggle to keep me on a reasonably
efficient track. So the issue is a highly sensitive one
to me for personal reasons. I know other people who
are much more self-assured and untroubled in this
area and who are admirably calm when faced with
one of my organizational hiccups.

How aware are you of the power your 'inner devil'
wields over your temper? You have nothing to lose
by taking a few minutes (in privacy!) to examine the
state of your soul.

**People in glasshouses should clean
their windows regularly if they want to
stay cool!**

**My father was often angry when
I was most like him.**

LILLIAN HELLMAN

Action time!

- **List your key general faults or weaknesses.** (For example, talking too much, swearing inappropriately, untidiness, procrastination, gossip, and so on.)

- **Make a list of six to ten mistakes you have made in your life.** (For example, choice of friend or partner, error of judgement at work, choosing the wrong question in an exam, over-committing yourself financially.)

- **Name some of the people that you have hurt emotionally in your life (either intentionally or otherwise).**

- **List a number of 'sins' you have committed during the last month.** These could be actions you have taken or not taken which are now a source of regret.

- **Remind yourself of some 'bad' thoughts you have had recently about people or about wrong actions you have been tempted to take.**

- **Restore the balance of your self-esteem** by giving yourself a small treat and reminding yourself of some of your strengths and achievements and/or taking some time out with a good friend who appreciates you ('warts and all'!).

STEP 6

Let go of the past you don't want

Stored emotional wounds can be lethally inflammable when anger is around. If you have a tendency to lose your cool, you must heal yours fast.

The following examples show how a spark of minor irritation can light an inferno when it falls on smouldering pain. Dan, Frankie and Bob's stories are very typical of those we hear so often in the anger management business:

- **Dan** was bullied throughout his childhood. He was picked on for being small and being poor. His memory of being laughed out of the playground when he wore hand-me-down shorts that crept unfashionably over his knees is as vivid as it ever was. As a result, the moment Dan thinks someone is demeaning him (and he thinks that often, even when it is patently untrue) his anger flares and his fight response kicks swiftly into action. He sought help after it had done that once too often with customers for the comfort of his company.

- **Frankie** has two young children, aged five and seven. Like any children of this age, they squabble over toys knocked over and whose knee to sit on. Frankie knows she loses her cool too readily when she hears them 'at it'. She wishes she could be like her friend, Tania, who can 'leave them to it'. But she can't, because the scenes press her own unhealed emotional buttons. Throughout her childhood she was the least shiny apple of her mother's eye. When she and her brothers quarrelled, she says, *'I was always the one that was given the blame. My mum used to say it was up to me as I was the oldest, I should know better.'*

- **Bob's** temper has lost him a string of girlfriends. He is now despairing of ever getting married again. Looking at the pattern behind his perpetual rows, it soon became obvious that his fear of being two-timed was fanning the flames of his fury. His first marriage broke up seven years earlier after his best friend tipped him off that his wife had been having an affair with another mutual friend for eighteen months. Instead of becoming appropriately angry, Bob blamed himself. He thought he had spent too much time away working and had not been appreciative enough of her. He claims to be the best of friends with both of them and says *'That's life for you. You win some and lose some – though I must say, I'm doing a bit of overtime on the losing side right now!'* Although there are some grains of truth in Bob's self-blame, his behaviour didn't warrant the kind of betrayal he encountered. He has to face and heal this hurt before he will be able to gain full control of his temper.

Are you still smarting from any old hurts or injustices? If so, it is time to do some emotional healing on those 'touchy subjects' that can throw you off balance. Of course you may never be able to rid yourself totally of all your past hurts. But if you do the following exercises, you will be able to keep the pain under *your* control.

In the past you may have had no choice about being hurt – but you can choose right NOW to heal yourself from the wound.

'The horror of that moment,' the King went on, 'I shall never forget.' 'You will though,' the Queen said, 'if you don't make a memorandum of it.'

LEWIS CARROLL

Action time!

- **List the key past hurts that are still emotionally painful enough to be hindering you from living your life to the full or are still affecting your behaviour.** (For example, bullying at school stops me from confronting bullies at work, being deceived in my first marriage makes me over-suspicious in relationships.)

- **Ask a friend to help you talk over these experiences in confidence.** Explain that you don't need advice – you just need to talk and express some feelings. Then, very importantly, let yourself be comforted by your friend – either through receiving a physical hug or listening attentively to their sympathy, or by allowing yourself to be cared for by them in another practical way, such as having a cup of tea or a pint of beer poured for you. (If you have expressed your hurt with real feeling and chosen the right friend, this comforting should come naturally – if it doesn't, move on and find another friend, or indeed a counsellor, who can give it to you.)

- **Find a way to compensate yourself.** This could be a generous treat to recompense yourself for the hurt, or it could be trying to find a replacement for what you lost (for example, a new friendship or good 'fathering' from a mentor at work or a sports coach).

- **Think about what you have gained from experiencing this hurt.** (For example, a new awareness of what you need in a relationship, a better understanding of yourself, more empathy with people who are having difficulties, and so on.)

STEP 7

Put yourself more firmly in the driving seat of your own life

Regret is also a highly inflammable feeling. It leaves us bitter and often cynical. And doesn't this hurt from a missed opportunity sting even more painfully when we know it was both avoidable and self-inflicted?

And to pile on the agony even more, regret can also lead to envy. This is yet another emotion which is often mishandled and affects our ability to stay cool.

If envy is used constructively, it can inspire us to achieve. But if it is kept hidden (or even half-denied), it can fester and then burst out in fits of sarcasm or temper. Sometimes venom is 'spat out' directly at the person we envy, but more commonly it surfaces as a 'niggle' which without our envy we would regard as trivial. In my first marriage, I secretly envied my husband's talent for writing. So, in spite of the fact that I genuinely wanted to support his creativity, I couldn't stop myself from flaring up when I saw him stop for a minute to jot down thoughts while in the middle of washing up or changing a nappy.

I am also convinced that regret and envy work their mischief at a subconscious level as well. Certainly, I have noticed a by-product of people starting to live the life they really want is that they automatically become much less prone to getting angry. Feeling a victim to life (especially one guaranteed 'to let you down in the end'!) keeps you in a negative state of mind. You are much more likely to see the worst rather than the best in any situation or person.

David is a good example of this truth in action. After a year of personal development work, he had negotiated a career plan for himself with his boss. They had agreed a detailed programme of training courses that the company would fund over the next five years. Nine months later, he went into the office to find a memo from his boss. It said that their budget had been drastically cut and David would no longer be eligible to attend more courses as the training quota had already been used up. Previously, he would have reacted by storming into his boss's office angrily waving the memo. But on this occasion he decided to take some time out to cool down and think before responding to this injustice. Once he had done so, he decided to explore some alternative options. He went to a head-hunter and found a position in another company, with an increased salary. The extra money was more than enough to enable him to fund his own way through MBA training. When David went to his boss with the news, the response he met was exactly what he needed (and deserved).

'Well done, David. I don't blame you. Wish I'd done the same myself years ago. Don't worry, you'll get a good reference from me. And don't forget, if things start looking up here again soon, we could be head-hunting you for a management post here.'

I appreciate that not everyone can do what David did when they meet such a problem, but perhaps there are other steps you could take which would give you a better sense of control over your life.

Taking charge of the overall direction of your life will breed a sense of personal power deep within you. Should your progress be frustrated, this power will make it easier for you to resist screaming into deaf ears. Instead, you can harness it to help you find an attractive alternative route.

**Regret for the things we did
can be tempered by time;
it is regret for the things we did
not do that is inconsolable.**

SYDNEY J. HARRIS

Action time!

- **Spend 10 to 15 minutes getting your body and mind into a deeply relaxed state** (see exercise on pages 96–99). Close your eyes and in your mind's eye form a vivid picture of yourself looking great at the age of 70. (This is a similar exercise to the one you did in Step 1, but it has some differences as you will see.)

- **Now imagine yourself being chauffeured to a TV studio in a large limousine.** You are going to be interviewed by a presenter for a very popular programme called *Achieving Your Life Dreams*. You have been chosen as an exemplary role model to appear in this programme! Think about what you might be telling the viewers about your life and the successes you have had.

- **Reflect on whether or not you believe these imagined dreams are at all achievable for you.** If they are not, modify them so that you can now write down three major long-term goals. (For example, run a successful business of your own, take a round-the-world trip, make a major difference to a charitable cause, create a happy family unit, and so on.)

- **Note down three things about yourself which are currently frustrating you from achieving these goals.** (For example, lack of forward-planning, laziness, fear of failure, over-spending, selfishness.)

- **Reflect on what you can do differently over the coming weeks to ensure that you get more of what you need and want out of life** (i.e. take some steps forward towards that life dream). Choose three of these to become your key resolutions. Write them out and pin them up where you and your supporters can see them.

STEP 8

Increase your physical energy

Our fuses light so much more easily when we are straining our bodies to the limits of their energy. Just think of how much less tolerant you feel when you are overtired, underfed, in pain or just struggling to keep going while coughing and sneezing your way through a cold.

Hopefully you will also agree quite readily that the opposite is also true. So I will assume that you don't need a lengthy sermon extolling the virtues of keeping your body in great shape. But on the understanding that most of us benefit from a gentle nudge in the direction we know we should be heading, I have included this step.

I am particularly aware of the relationship between the physical care of our bodies and our temper because I am writing this a week or two before Christmas. This is a time when I get endless phone calls from journalists who are ringing me for advice to give to their readers on how to keep their cool at Christmas. Of course, there are many causes of family tension at Christmas, and each household has its own unique, complex concoction of these. But one of the main reasons why tempers erupt at this festive time has to do with the state of the bodies of at least one of the people involved!

Christmas is a time when people are commonly worn out by the extra demands of shopping, partying, worrying, sleep deprivation and overindulgence. In short, our bodies are stressed. So the slightest prick to our pride or the smallest frustration or annoyance can burst the fragile, happy bubble that society does its best to cocoon us in. But the good thing about Christmas, in comparison to many other stressful periods that life can bring, is that we know when it is coming. So the short-fused amongst us always need to make sure that we are in extra-good physical shape before it arrives.

How stress-proof is your body? Could it withstand the Christmas pressure test right now? None of us can ever be sure when an unexpected challenge might put extra demands on our energy.

Aim to keep your body in the kind of shape *today* that it might need to be in tomorrow.

It is in the living body where the real magic lies – magic that can bring you smoother skin, more energy, a leaner, firmer body, better hormone balance, greater stamina, as well as better emotional balance and a new sense of freedom 'to be who you are' with ease.

LESLIE KENTON

Action time!

- **Unless you have had one very recently, make an appointment** *right now* **(or, at the latest, by the end of tomorrow!) to have a health and fitness check.** Your own doctor, a commercial health insurance company or a fitness trainer can do this. You may also want to include a trip to the dentist. Bad teeth not only can cause irritation and pain in our mouths, but also in our digestive systems. Their infections can also depress our immune system and sap our energy long before we are aware of any pain. (I learned this bit of dental wisdom the hard way!)

- **Even if you have been given a clean bill of health by your expert, vow to give yourself a basic DIY check every month by asking yourself the following questions.** If you are statistically minded, it might be useful to give yourself a rating on a scale of 1–10 for each. You will obviously have to add to these questions (or adapt them) if your doctor or fitness instructor has diagnosed a specific problem.

During the last month:

– *What proportion of nights have I had adequate sleep?* (Six to eight hours per night for most mortals!)

– *Have I eaten healthily enough?* (For example, adequate fresh fruit and vegetables each day, kept 'sinful' fatty and sugary foods as rare treats, and so forth.)

– *Have I drunk enough of what is good for me and said 'no' enough to toxic drinks?* (For example, minimum of two litres of pure water per day, maximum of two cups of tea or coffee per day, maximum of two to three units of alcohol per day.)

– *Have I exercised enough?* (For example, stretched tense muscles once an hour, undertaken 20 minutes of aerobic exercise per week.)

Stage Three

retraining your auto-responses

As I said earlier, this stage is the heart of the Shortcut strategy. It is about replacing the unhelpful 'fight/flight/freeze' responses which are programmed into your subconscious through your genes, early childhood experiences or traumatic events in your adult life, by 'over-writing' them with new, assertive, safe ones. Each of its steps is full of practical work. Some contain guidelines and techniques which you will need to learn by heart and repeat constantly before you can expect good results. You may find it helpful to photocopy these so that you can refer to them easily when you meet real-life tests.

**Think you can, think you can't;
either way, you'll be right.**

HENRY FORD

STEP 9

Think positively in the face of difficult challenges

One of the most moving (and humbling) experiences of my life was a visit I made to Robben Island, off the coast of South Africa, where Nelson Mandela and hundreds of others were imprisoned for so many years. My daughter bought me a mouse mat from the museum there as a memento. On it is printed this quotation from Ahmed Kathrada, who was imprisoned on the island for 25 years.

'While we will not forget the brutality of apartheid, we will not want Robben Island to be a monument of our hardship and suffering. We would want it to be a triumph of the human spirit against the forces of evil; a triumph of wisdom and largeness of spirit against small minds and pettiness; a triumph of courage and determination over human frailty and weakness.'

Every day it reminds me of the potentially ennobling and life-enhancing qualities of difficult challenges. My own (like yours, I hope) have never been on the scale of the apartheid challenge, but there have been plenty where I knew that in order to 'right the wrong' which I saw, I would inevitably meet resistance and even encounter dislike. (For example, when I was campaigning against selfish parking in our neighbourhood or challenging disrespectful and unjust psychiatric practices on behalf of my clients.)

Even though I have worked long and hard at taming my personality, under the stress of a frustrating setback I still feel automatically compelled to rant and rage against the 'culprit'. When this happens I use positive thinking 'tricks', such as glancing at my mouse mat, to keep this auto-response in hand. Doing this has controlled many an intense urge to 'smash some sense' into my stubborn computer!

If you are reading this book, it is likely that you have been pre-programmed to see most challenges as threats. A fair proportion of these may indeed be real threats. But, nevertheless, you have probably been 'set-up' by your genes or subconscious conditioning to see even these as larger or less resolvable than they actually are. Positive thinking strategies will help you to counter this emotional conditioning and help you to gain a more rational and optimistic perspective.

> **Optimism will keep you in the frame of mind that will notice the opportunities even in hurtful and unfair situations.**

Action time!

- **Choose three or four quotations from this book which you think could encourage you to respond to challenge more positively.** (Or find alternatives from other books, such as those suggested in the Recommended Reading section at the end of the book.) Write or print these out and pin them up in places where you will see them each day. You could stick them on your computer or fridge door as I often do, or you could even treat yourself to a full colour poster or have them printed on a new mug or coaster. Make a point of reading these quotations (out loud if you can) at least once a day. Change your quotations every few months. By the end of that period they should have been stored in your unconscious brain and you can enjoy searching for some new ones.

- **Think of a current difficult challenge which is making you feel frustrated or angry.** (A past or imaginary one would do as a passable second-best!)

    Ask yourself the following questions. (Use the help of a level-headed friend or colleague if you suspect your feelings are already so strong that they could be interfering with your rational thinking ability.)

1. How would ___ (select one of your heroes – alive, dead or from fiction) have responded to this challenge?
2. What is the exact real threat in this challenge? (We almost always exaggerate this when we are angry.)
3. What are some of the positive qualities in the people who are causing/contributing to the problem?
4. What could I learn from dealing with this problem?
5. Are there any other potentially positive outcomes or opportunities that could result from this challenge?

STEP 10

Become aware of when your auto-response is triggering difficult behaviour in others

Please notice that I am not using the now common term 'difficult people'. This is because I hate it! (And it triggers my anger!) Using a negative 'label' such as this only creates additional problems, and is, arguably, arrogant and often downright unfair. Now I had better cool down and offer you some explanation!

When you use such a term you are setting up your brain to highlight the faults in the other person and you will automatically feel defensive in their presence. Even if you never use the term in front of the person concerned, by articulating it in your head or with others you are prejudicing your subconscious mind against them.

Another reason for avoiding this term is that it puts the 'blame' too firmly on 'the other person'. The truth is that some people are likely to find your 'difficult' people very 'easy' indeed (*even* if many around you share your view of them). The chances are that at least some part of the responsibility for the problem *could* be yours. (And isn't this book designed to help you change aspects of *your* behaviour and not to work miracles on others?!)

You could, for example, be prejudging a person in a negative way because you are harbouring 'prejudices'. None of us likes to admit that we may do this, but a stark psychological fact is that we all do. We cannot help doing so. Our brain does the job automatically for us. For example, if your senses pick up a familiar tone of voice, hair colour or a particular phrase which has hurtful or fearful connotations for you (based on one of your past experiences or your cultural conditioning), they will alert your brain and you will automatically be put into 'on guard' mode. This will affect your perception and mean that you are more likely to notice the negative aspects of that person.

You could also be unconsciously forming a prejudice against a person if your first meeting with them took place while you were in a bad mood or if they happened to be the messenger of bad news. Research has proved that these powerful first impressions are very hard to shift.

When your mind is 'set' against a person (even without your conscious consent) **not only does that affect the way you perceive them, very often it also affects how they respond to you.** Some people's brains in particular are very adept at sensing hidden hostility, even if this hostility is masked with smiles and sweet words. When this happens they are automatically put into defensive mode. They may even realize that they are being 'guarded' or 'prickly' with you, but not understand why. And so begins a vicious cycle that can quickly escalate and be revealed in inappropriate friction over petty concerns.

Alternatively, some of the 'blame' for the problem could lie in the way you are unconsciously communicating with the other person. In an ideal world we would all continually adapt the way we talk and use our body language to fit with each individual we meet. Perhaps you already try very hard to do so. But few of us actually achieve this. (We are human, after all!) Instead, most of the time in our busy everyday lives we rarely *consciously think* and appraise the other person before we talk or move our body. Our subconscious does the job for us. For quick processing, it 'chunks' people or situations together in our minds and then 'shapes' our communication style accordingly. For example, your brain will have stored one dominant communication style for your neighbours which is different from the one it has stored for you to use with people inside your home.

But that's not all, I'm afraid. **Aspects of your personality or behaviour or the role that you are in also play their part in this subconscious merry-go-round.** They may act as an automatic trigger to the other person to act in a frustrating or hurtful way with you. For example, most 'nice policemen' and 'nice head teachers' soon find out that many people cower into frustrating timidity the moment they see them. (Perhaps these people had one too many detentions at school!)

Of course (in that ideal world again!), people who behave in a difficult way ought to control their own triggers. But the reality we have to work with is that many do not. So, that leaves us with a choice:

- to either continue as before (i.e. blaming other people for being difficult and carrying on losing our cool with them in the hope they will get the message *one* day)

or,

- to acknowledge and try to modify some of our subconscious 'triggers'

You may not think it is always strictly 'fair' to suggest the latter option. But for *your* own sake (or peace's sake), might it not be worth giving this kind of injustice an occasional go?

The workings of your subconscious mind on others is always *your* responsibility.

**Curious things habits.
People themselves never
knew they had them.**

AGATHA CHRISTIE

Action time!

- **Write a list of the types of people you find difficult and also name some specific people.**

- **Think about some of the unpleasant experiences you received in your early childhood and the people who you found difficult then.** (Even petty displeasures and innocuous people in childhood can have a formative impact on your subconscious mind. If they are powerfully vivid in your memory, trust that they may still be significant.)

- **Think also about some of the unpleasant experiences you have received in adulthood at the hands of other people.** (Remember, that to create a 'prejudice' in adulthood, these need to have been *very* or *repeatedly* unpleasant.)

- **Name some of the major roles you have in your life in relation to people.** (For example, father, mother, boyfriend, girlfriend, coach, advisor, and so on.)

- **List your key dominant personality traits** –
  the ones which 'hit' people the moment they
  meet you. (For example, friendliness, directness,
  compassion, earnestness, and so on.)

- **Now, look again at the first list of people you
  find 'difficult' and see if you can make any
  connections with the other lists.** For example:

  – *Could the similarities between my infuriatingly
  unassertive mother and 'Dormouse Dawn' in the
  accounts office be triggering her to be so irritat-
  ingly unforthcoming with me?*
  – *Could my supervisory role with John be helping to
  put him on the defensive?*
  – *Could my overly-trusting nature be triggering my
  sister's jealousy?*

- **Focus on what you could try to do to help the
  situation.** You may find that just reminding
  yourself of your potential unconscious triggers
  will make an immediate improvement, but you
  could also consider discussing your thoughts
  with the other person or a trusted friend or
  mentor. Even if the connections you have made
  are way off the mark, at least you are indicating

a willingness to take *some* responsibility, and doing this may kick-start a negotiation. By insisting that the focus stays on *what can be done differently*, you can avoid the discussion deteriorating into a 'blame game'.

STEP 11

Feed your conscience with crystal-clear firing instructions

Now it's time to give the conscious logical thinking and moral powers of your mind some attention. You have seen how your subconscious may cause your anger to 'fire off' without your permission and we have looked at some ways to control this. This step will also help this problem in a more indirect way. By consciously allowing yourself some legitimate targets for your anger energy, you will find yourself less at the mercy of your subconscious. But that particular outcome is a by-product of this step's work rather than its core objective. The central aim of this step is to help you use your capacity for anger in a safe, purposeful and powerfully effective way by making sure it stays focussed on achievable goals.

As you know, I like and respect my anger. It gives me the energy and courage to do the 'right' thing by my conscience when the coward in me is scared of 'making a fuss' or being disliked. But for many years in my early adulthood it was unquestionably a 'loose cannon'.

After discovering through therapy that my crippling depressive episodes were frequently fuelled by unexpressed, justified anger, I began to fire off randomly at any and every frustration and injustice that tickled my indignation. In my work with the mentally ill, my anger was particularly effective. It helped me successfully 'fight' many a battle with bureaucracy on behalf of inarticulate clients. But I was burning out fast and my personal relationships were disintegrating.

Eventually, after a spate of spectacularly self-destructive and hurtful shooting of venom, I took some time out for a serious one-to-one with my conscience. As a result, I was able to accept that, however defensible my anger was, by allowing it to fire off so indiscriminately I was doing more harm than good to the issues I cared about. When I started to be more selective about my targets I found that not only did my health improve, but also my anger became a more effective tool for instigating the changes I wanted to see.

Don't you find you listen more attentively when a generally calm person is protesting with passion than to someone who is sounding off continually?

These next exercises will help you to clarify in your conscious mind which are your own *current* prime targets. In doing this, you will be giving yourself permission to stay *feeling* angry when you encounter certain frustrations, hurts and injustices. **But please bear in mind that you are not necessarily *yet* qualified to 'shoot'. The art and skill of expressing your anger safely and skilfully will be covered in subsequent steps.**

Take pride in your conscience and use targeted anger to make it work constructively for you and your causes.

**It is in self-limitation
that a master first shows himself.**

JOHANN VON GOETHE

Action time!

• **Read and learn by heart the 'Reminder' on page 90,** which I have adapted from Reinhold Niebuhr's 'Serenity Prayer'. It has become a constant mantra in my own head. Nowadays (more often than not!), it automatically pops into my conscious mind just as my anger fuse begins to ignite. I can highly recommend its energy-saving qualities.

• **Start preparing a personal 'Conscience Charter' for yourself.** In a notebook or on your computer, create three sections for recording any issue or happening which causes you (or could cause you) to feel some degree of moral outrage. You may become aware of these through your real-life encounters or you could come across them while doing something, such as reading the paper or watching the news or a Soap on TV. (You will not have to do this forever and ever, but merely until you have mastered the habit of anger targeting.)

Enter each issue under the appropriate heading. Take care to be guided by your *own* conscience.

1. mini-matters
2. medium-matters
3. mega-matters

- **Use the above lists each month to help you identify more specifically those matters that are *currently* bugging you on a day-to-day basis.** Choose approximately six to ten of these that you would like to concentrate on staying cool over during the next month or two. Bear in mind the importance of the issue, but also your schedule and energy levels. (The 'Serenity Prayer' may also help make a hard choice easier!) Make a list similar to the one below.

This month's 'Keep Cool' list:
– trains running up to ten-minutes late
– traffic jams of all kinds
– children swearing
– socks on the bedroom floor
– e-mail shutdowns
– biased news items

In Step 12 you will be learning some techniques to help you master the art of pulse control – once you have learned these and are feeling

more relaxed, you might want to add a couple
more examples to your list.

- **List a similar number of key matters which
  are bugging you on a day-to-day basis – and
  that you will give yourself full permission to
  pursue once you have finished this strategy.**
  When compiling the list, again take care to be
  realistic in your selection. Be aware that it is
  always best to practise new behaviour on smaller
  matters and be honest about the amount of
  energy and time you want to *currently* spare –
  otherwise you will lose your cool with yourself
  for not achieving the impossible!

This month's 'Anger Targets' list could look
something like this:

  – inefficiency on the railways
  – unequal opportunity at work
  – abusive customers
  – school bullies
  – office gossips
  – wanton destruction of the environment

REMINDER!

In order to keep my cool, I must:
accept the things which cannot
be changed,
have the courage to change the things
that I want to change,
and have the wisdom to distinguish
one from the other.

ADAPTED FROM 'THE SERENITY PRAYER',
ATTRIBUTED TO REINHOLD NIEBUHR

STEP 12

Master the art of pulse control

This step is about gaining control over the bio-chemical changes that take place in your body once your anger is triggered. At the start of this strategy we looked briefly at how the anger response works physiologically. You will recall that once it kicks into action, hormones are produced which raise our pulse rate and make our heart work in a faster gear. Remember the 'Jungle Speedway' and the 'Wisdom Way' routes? (If not, re-read page 20 now to refresh your memory.)

If you have been diligently following the suggestions in the previous steps, you should be feeling calm a good deal more often. Can I assume that, at the very least, you are eating and drinking more carefully, exercising more regularly, keeping your self-esteem boosted, thinking positively and giving yourself more time for reflection and planning? So you should have noticed that your pulse is now less likely to soar at the slightest provocation.

But, unfortunately, we fiery people need to do a little more than just adopt this calming lifestyle. We also need to take more direct action, especially when we know we are living with an over-abundance of frustration and pressure.

My own recommendation is that we should ensure that we:

– make a habit of doing **5-minute breathing exercises** at regular intervals throughout each day (see pages 95–96)
– experience a **15-minute period of deep relaxation** at least twice a week (see pages 96–99)
– employ one well-rehearsed **defusing technique** as soon as we become aware that our anger has been triggered, or we think that there is a chance that it could be (see pages 99–102)

If you felt the need to read this book it is unlikely that you do *any* of these things. (Well, to a good-enough standard anyway!) I have found that everyone with whom I have worked has needed help in these areas. Before turning to me, most have already tried very hard to calm themselves down. So, understandably, they have a very negative view of the power of relaxation to help.

Perhaps you are feeling similarly. If so, I can only suggest that you, too, give your body another chance. Unless for some reason you have a physical or mental impairment that makes it impossible for you to do these exercises, try trusting that you *can* exert control over your pulse rate. The belief that it *is* possible is more than half the battle. The techniques themselves are so easy to learn and do. ('The simpler the better' is a golden rule when sending signals to the primitive emotional centre in our brain which is responsible for producing the hormones that start our pulses racing.)

> **Trust that controlling your pulse is easy – and it will be!**

Action time!

- **Set aside time in your diary to rehearse the following three exercises several times over the next few weeks.** Make sure that you have privacy and a quiet place to practise in at first. Once you have trained your brain to respond, you should be able to do the exercises almost anywhere, at any time. The more often you do them, the quicker your pulse will respond. Some people find they are more inspired if they can actually *see* the evidence. There are now many different kinds of small machines which indicate the effect of relaxation on blood pressure flow. If you think one would help you, ask your doctor or health clinic to recommend where you can buy or borrow a reliable small monitor for your own use at home.

  If you find that these self-help exercises still have no effect on your pulse rate, try some others. There are literally hundreds and hundreds more which might do the trick for you. (See the Further Help section for just a few books and tapes on the subject.) Alternatively, consult a local stress specialist. Again, it is advisable to ask your doctor or other reliable person for a recommendation or a referral. (Many stress specialists who advertise have limited training and may not be skilled enough to break through your resistance.)

5-MINUTE BREATHER

You can do this exercise wherever you are and whether you are lying, sitting or standing – but if you can, steady yourself first by putting both feet on the ground. Also, unclench any muscles you may be holding in a tight position (for example, uncross your legs or arms).

While keeping your focus on the passage of air as it goes through your body:

- Slowly breathe in through your nose, expanding your lungs as fully as you can, pushing your diaphragm down and your stomach out.
- Hold your breath for five to ten seconds.
- Exhale slowly through your mouth while lifting your diaphragm and bringing your stomach in.
- Repeat several times, each time taking slightly longer to complete the cycle and trying to keep the passage of air flowing at a steady, even rate.

– Now, as you breathe in, imagine that you are inhaling a bright white-coloured energy. Then, as you breathe out, imagine that you are exhaling air that has a pale-blue glow. Every time a thought comes into your mind, return the focus of your attention to the colour you should be visualizing as you breathe in and out.

15-MINUTE DEEP RELAXATION EXERCISE

This method of relaxation is achieved by firstly contracting and then relaxing each of the major muscle groups in turn. This allows you to feel the difference between contraction (tension) and relaxation. The idea is that, in the end, you will be able to relax your muscles without going through the contracting phase, as you will know what the difference feels like. However, this may take some time.

Remember while you are doing the exercise to keep your breathing deep, slow and regular. Most people find it easier to practise this technique if they are lying down (with arms lying by the side of the body, legs slightly apart), but it is also a good idea to practise in a sitting position.

You can ask someone with a soothing voice to read out the instructions. Alternatively, you can record them yourself onto a tape with your favourite relaxing music or sounds in the background.

Now start your relaxation:

Facial muscles
- Lift your eyebrows upwards as high as they will go, and then relax them.
- Close your eyes tight, as tightly as you possibly can, and then relax them.
- Curl your upper lip up to your nose. Feel the tension, then relax it.
- Curl your lower lip down towards your chin, and then relax it.
- Curl up your tongue in your mouth, and then relax it.
- Clench your teeth, then relax them.
- Push your jaw forward and backwards.

Upper body muscles
- Bend your chin forward to touch your chest, and then relax it. Push your head backwards – as far back as it will go – then relax. Turn your head to the left – then relax. Turn your head to the right. Relax.

- Shrug your shoulders as high up as they will go. Relax. Push your shoulder blades back. Relax. Bring your shoulders forward. Relax.

Upper limbs
- Press your arms into your sides, as tightly as you can. Relax. Bend your arms at the elbows. Squeeze as tight as you can. Relax.
- Bend your wrists backwards as far as they will go. Relax.
- Clench your hands as tight as you can. Relax.

Check that you are breathing deeply and slowly.

Stomach and pelvic muscles
- Pull your stomach in as tightly as you can. Relax.
- Contract your anal and pelvic muscles as tightly as you can. Relax.

Lower limbs
- Bring your left knee to your chest as tightly as you can. Relax.
- Bring your right knee to your chest as tightly as you can. Relax.
- With bent knees, press both knees together as tightly as you can. Relax.

- Bend your heels backwards as far as you can. Relax.
- Stretch your feet forward as tightly as you can. Relax.
- Curl your toes up as tightly as you can. Relax.

Lie relaxed for as many minutes as you can spare. Then, when you sense your energy returning, start to move your body gently and leisurely stretch your limbs. Never get upsuddenly. Rather, do so slowly and carefully.

TEMPER DEFUSER

Use this strategy as soon as you begin to feel anger taking a hold in your body. In taking each of the following steps you are, in effect, sending 'switch-off' signals to the 'fight/flight/freeze' centre in your emotional brain which in turn will slow down the rate of your pulse.

1. *Establish some DISTANCE from your anger trigger*
   For example, you could take a step back, lean back in a chair, leave the room, or say to them or yourself that you will 'sleep on it'.

2. *Become more GROUNDED*

First, do this quite literally by putting both feet on the ground and taking hold of some firm, inanimate object such as a chair or table. Secondly, switch yourself out of your emotional right-brain mode by bringing yourself back 'down to earth' with a mundane chore. You could, for example, count all the blue or circular objects in the room, or compose a shopping list for a particular meal, or calmly recite the words of a song or poem you know. Then, if you have time, for the next 20 minutes engage yourself in an absorbing and distracting routine task, such as doing some easy administrative work or cleaning or gardening. (This is how long it takes for your pulse to return to normal functioning.)

3. *Release some TENSION*

At the very least, clench and slowly unclench your fists or toes. You can usually do either without anyone seeing! If you can get some privacy, screw your face and body up and release the muscles slowly a few times. If you are still very tense and have time, go for a run or a swim. Alternatively, find a secluded spot where you could kick a cushion around for a *few* minutes while letting out some deep growls. (But don't do this for so long that you make your pulse start to race again. And *never* pretend that the cushion is a person.)

4. *Take control of your BREATH*
Before saying or doing anything about the trigger (or indeed anything else of importance), use the five-minute breathing exercise (see pages 95–96) to control the flow of your breath. Check that you are breathing from your diaphragm and not your upper chest. (When we start to get angry we begin to breathe much more quickly and less deeply. This has a quickening effect on our pulse.)

You can quickly remind yourself of the above four steps by saying '**D**on't **G**et **T**oo **B**oiling' as soon as your pulse rate starts to change. Notice how the first letter of each word in this sentence is the same as the key words highlighted in the headings of each task I have listed above. Why not copy page 102 as a reminder and pin it up somewhere until it is well fixed in your memory.

Don't **G**et **T**oo **B**oiling
I   **R**   **E**   **R**
S   **O**   **E**   **E**
T   **U**   **N**   **A**
A   **N**   **S**   **T**
N   **D**   **I**   **H**
C   **E**   **O**
E   **D**   **N**

STEP 13

Tone down your talk

This is a tall order, but it is especially important for the overtly passionate amongst us! (I will address the needs of you quieter types later!)

As I mentioned in Step 10, **most of the time when we are communicating we are operating in auto-pilot mode.** You are probably not aware of just how many unnecessary exaggerations, aggressive sarcastic quips, grandiose 'sermons' and threatening gestures you are using. (And you may also not realize how many pulses, including your own, start racing when you do use them.)

This is why you will need to enlist some help for this step. It requires people to tell you when you are getting the talk right and when you are getting it wrong. As it may well involve them interrupting you while you are in 'full flow', you must ensure that these are the kind of people who aren't too intimidated by your colourful style!

At first you may resist. You will probably hate the feeling of not sounding like 'you'. Changing the way you talk may even seem quite threatening because it can feel as though you are in danger of becoming a rather dull and colourless person. Although it sounds quite arrogant, I admit that is exactly how I responded at first and I have seen many other people react similarly. You may need to remind yourself that you are not just your 'talk', and that you are still the deep meaningful you! This step is, after all, only designed to help you modify an aspect of your *learned* behaviour (one you know which keeps you swimming in far too much hot water than you can currently handle). Once you have mastered your temper you can return to using as much wildly colourful language as you like. (As long as you are prepared to take on any triggered consequences!)

There are several reasons why I recommend modifying your language. Firstly, because it is relatively easy to do. It doesn't take much effort, skill, memory or time just to experiment with changing a few words or one aspect of your body language. Secondly, it usually gets surprisingly quick and inspiring results. Most people are amazed at the effect that such a simple change can have on their feelings and other people's responses. Thirdly, it heightens our awareness. Even sounding or feeling a little different from usual helps keep us operating more often in conscious mode. We are therefore less liable to be triggered into the auto-responses which may have been previously causing us trouble (as discussed in Step 10).

But why should the more reserved amongst us also need this step? Unless you are the exception I have never yet met, I believe that you 'quiet types' do also have a propensity for colourful language. But perhaps your only witnesses are those who see you losing your cool, or those who can read your mind! You may not need to tone down your everyday spoken language, but you could probably do with watching your self-talk, body language and written communication. (All can have nearly as much pulse-racing potential as loud, flamboyant speech.) You may also need to refer to the following boxes in the Action Time! section while you are doing the exercises in Step 14, which involve preparing and rehearsing assertive anger responses.

So, I'm afraid, no one who loses their cool should let themselves off this hook!

> **Tamer talk won't kill the passionate side of you – it will simply harness it so you can use it when *you* choose to do so.**

**Thanks to words, we have been
able to rise above brutes;
and thanks to words, we have often
sunk to the level of demons.**

ALDOUS HUXLEY

Action time!

- **Read the 'Language to Curb' examples on pages 109–111**, either aloud or in your head, and mark the words and phrases that you tend to use. Do the same with the 'Body Language to Cut' examples on page 111. Then add to the lists your own variations and favourites. There are obviously thousands of variables on these themes. Select no more than six words, two phrases and two examples of body language you want to try to stop using over the next two weeks.

- **Study the examples of commonly accepted assertive language** (see pages 112–114) **and body language** (see page 114). Again, there are many regional and cultural variables so you can add your own examples, but it may be useful to ask a calm, assertive friend for advice. For each of the words, phrases and body language examples you want to stop using find an alternative assertive or toned-down word or phrase – or alternative body language – you can try instead. Share your intention with several people who can and are willing to help.

Getting the talk wrong ...

Here are some examples of common words and phrases that people tend to use in their everyday language. As you will see, the pulse-racing potential of each is enormous!

LANGUAGE TO CURB
Exaggerated exaggerations
always

appalling

awful

completely

insufferable

totally

never

I can't bear it a minute longer ...

It's mind-blowingly obvious

That's just a load of drivel

He's a totally ignorant ...

You're a complete twit/idiot

Get lost – and don't ever come back

You make me sick

We'll be there all night if that goes on the agenda
Nobody around here ever listens/cares/helps

Grandiose sermonizing

They ought to get their act together
The only answer is ...
Who do they think they are?
You should never, ever ...
... and that's the end of it!
I've lived a hell of a lot longer than you!
It's right because I said so

Over-generalized labelling

You women/men ...
You teenagers always ...
That's Irish blarney!
Your Mediterranean temper is off again
That's typical accountant/lawyer/politician talk!
Don't give me any of that psychobabble

Unrealistic threats

I'll never speak to you again
I'll flatten you
You'll be the death of me
To hell with you

Just you wait ... you won't know what hit you
I'll be dead and buried by the time you ...

Swear words and obscenities
       Each and every one of them!

BODY LANGUAGE TO CUT

clenched fists/waving fists in air/banging fists onto
a hard surface
pointing or tapping fingers
hands on hips
dramatic folding of arms and legs
raised, sarcastic or mimicking tone of voice
staring and glaring
rigid posture
encroaching on personal space (uninvited)
sarcastic smiling/frowning/raised eyebrows
sneering and sniggering
tossing back of head
putting hands on head or over ears
looking down while shaking head
peering pointedly over glasses
dramatically looking away or up

Getting the talk right ...

Now let's look at some examples of assertive anger language and body language you can use to help you – and other people – stay cool.

ASSERTIVE ANGER LANGUAGE

Empathizing

I don't mean to hurt you, but I want you to know that ...
I appreciate your point, but ...
I can see that you are very concerned, but ...

Stating and owning feelings (rather than blaming)

I'm feeling myself getting a bit irritated, could we please try ...?
At the moment I'm too angry to think clearly or discuss calmly ...
I'm getting so keyed up that I'd better cool off before carrying on. Can I give you a ring on ...?

Clarifying contract and responsibility

I know that I let you down over ... , but you did promise to ...
We agreed that we would both ... I have, but, as yet, you have not ...

Yes, I did promise but failed you. I am sorry. You have a right to feel letdown.

To make amends can I suggest …?

Setting limits

I don't like leaving this matter unresolved, but suggest that we agree to postpone our decision until …

I am prepared to negotiate over … but not on …

I understand that you would like … but that has to be my bottom line on these issues because …

Highlighting common ground

Let's see if we can agree on some …

Shall we start with the common ground between us? We both want to … And neither of us likes …

Can we both beg to differ on that one?

Keeping grounded

This is simply my opinion, but I'd like you to hear it nevertheless … What do you think?

I'd like to stick to the facts which, as I see them, are …

The actual figures here state that …

I have actually been late on three out of eighteen occasions in the last month.

Moving on

Can we look at what we have learned from this?

We have only 10 minutes left, so I would like to confirm what we have agreed and the outstanding differences. Then we can settle on the next step.

We are both still feeling very angry. I suggest that we sleep on it and then ...

Perhaps we have reached stalemate and it is time for a third party to help.

We may not have reached agreement on ... but at least we did ...

ASSERTIVE BODY LANGUAGE

relaxed, open, upright posture

when listening, head slightly tilted to side and nodding

both feet on the ground

hands loosely placed at side or together on table (no fiddling!)

strong, medium-toned and level voice

serious facial expression

direct eye contact

keeping distance (by leaning back in chair or taking small step back)

STEP 14

Repeatedly rehearse assertive responses

As I write this, New Year resolution time is fast approaching. No doubt many people will be once again vowing to change at least one of their 'bad' behaviours over the coming few months. The sad truth is that many of them will once again be disappointed with themselves. They will fail simply because they have relied too heavily on their good intention to 'do the trick'. Unfortunately, there is no magic involved in the business of personal transformation. No amount of wishful thinking can budge bad habits.

If you want to imbed an alternative habitual response into your personality, your motivation must be backed up with a **mundane step-by-step action plan.** (Though this should, of course, include an abundance of treats for good behaviour!) This plan must ensure that your new response can be *practised* over and over again. Research has revealed that it generally takes at least 20 repetitions of new behaviour – plus 20 immediate rewards – in fairly rapid succession before there is any hope that it will become fixed as a neurological 'pattern' in our brain. But, unfortunately, I have found that it takes even more than this number to replace a long-established anger habit.

It is pretty obvious that it is neither practical nor advisable to wait for real life to come up with opportunities to practise more assertive (rather than aggressive) anger responses. (Are you usually in the mood for experimenting when you are losing your cool?) You need to create a mock environment where you can rehearse in privacy and safety. There are a variety of ways you can do this, as you will see in the following suggestions. Choose at least one of the options and make sure that enough rehearsal time gets firmly scheduled into your diary. (Aim to practise a few key responses in one form or another over the next month. By then it should be established as a habit.)

Assertive behaviour – just like angry behaviour – is only a habit. But like any other habit it needs repetition to fix it firmly in place.

Character is built into the spiritual
fabric of the personality
hour by hour, day by day, year by year
in much the same deliberate way
that physical health is built
into the body.

E. LAMAR KINCAID

Action time!

- **Think of three examples of when you have lost your cool.** Choose ones which are as recent as possible and in differing situations. Write down some of the key phrases, looks or sentences which triggered your angry response. Beside each, write down an assertive response which you could have used instead. (Aim to make a list of about ten sentences. It doesn't matter if you cannot remember the language exactly.) Use the examples in Step 13 to guide you. Practise saying these out loud, watching yourself carefully in the mirror every day for the next week. You could stick the list on a mirror you use each morning to remind yourself.

- **Ask a friend to have a role-playing session with you.** Get them to feed you with some triggers while you practise responding assertively. It can be more fun (and helpful) to get them to 'up the tempo' with exaggerated verbal and non-verbal triggers – but take care not to become really angry! You could also discuss the defusing strategy in Step 12 and how you would put it into effect.

- **Use the creative visualization technique we used in Step 1 to fix an image in your brain of you handling the above situations in a very calm, assertive manner.**

- **Make it a habit to use these techniques in a preventative way.** The next time you think you will be in a situation which you know might raise your hackles, make sure that you do at least one of the above.

- **Make a list of rewards you could give yourself when you notice an improvement in your behaviour.** (Don't forget you can reward even a slight step forward!)

- **Join an assertiveness training class and ask assertively for some practice on your anger responses!**

STEP 15

Lessen your fear of other people's anger

Perhaps the most difficult temper trigger of all is other people's anger. This is because an auto-response is so deeply embedded in our genetic programming. The moment we notice someone else is angry with us, our brain 'sees red' and switches on its alarm mode. For those of us with a short fuse this will most likely be the 'fight' rather than the 'flight' or 'freeze' option. (And don't forget this will happen even if the other person's anger is displayed in a passive rather than aggressive way.)

But although this is the most challenging trigger, it nevertheless isn't *impossible* to manage. We can and must do more than just suppress our temper. I make this point because I have seen many too many people limit their lives and give themselves unnecessary angst because they believe this is their only option. For example, in their effort to 'keep the peace' and keep control of their own feelings they:

- are careful not to stick their neck out at work with bullying colleagues so they and their needs get continually overlooked
- will not assert themselves with 'bolshy', irate customers so their self-esteem plummets and they become generally cynical about mankind
- don't argue back with irritable partners and cynical friends so they put up with third- or fourth-class personal relationships and a boring personal life
- hold back from complaining to sullen waiters so they eat cold and unpalatable food and run the risk of getting food poisoning
- let their argumentative young children 'walk all over' them so they set themselves up for teen trouble

Are you paying too big a price for keeping other people cool?

I am not advocating that you start training as a matador and take to waving red flags back at them.

In fact, I firmly believe that everyone should stay wary of both the dangerous 'raging bulls' and the sly 'rats' in their world! In situations where we obviously have very little power to defend ourselves and are physically threatened, we have a right to run away and fetch back the most powerful 'army' we can find to help us. (The 'army' could be any person or people whom you can trust to defend you.)

But such extreme dangers are rare. As a general rule, we should not swallow our own feelings, sit back in fear and watch other people's anger ruin our lives. We need to develop the courage to do what we can without endangering our lives and limbs or endangering anyone else either. If we don't, our own pent-up fear and anger could burst through in temper when we least want it to do so.

And now for some good news!

You have done at least 90% of the work for this step already! Learning how to stay cool and express your own anger assertively are the golden keys to managing other people's temper.

> Don't swallow your fear and watch other people's anger ruin your life. Instead, convert it into courage and use your *own* anger assertively to get what you need and want.

**Bravery is the capacity to
perform properly,
Even when scared half to death.**

GENERAL OMAR N. BRADLEY

Action time!

- **Read the following suggestions and the sample script on page 128 for defusing someone else's anger, and rehearse them repeatedly** (as discussed in Step 14).

  When faced with someone who is losing their cool:

  – Breathe, breathe and breathe again before doing anything. Take a few minutes to do the exercise on pages 95–96 if you can.
  – Adopt an assertive, upright, relaxed posture and maintain direct eye-contact (see page 114).
  – Take a small, firm step back or lean back slightly (to send a 'no fight here' signal to their emotional brain).
  – Steady and ground yourself by holding onto something solid such as a table, door or the car roof.
  – Talk calmingly and encouragingly to yourself. (In silence, of course!) For example: *'I am calm ... I can cope ... I can defuse this ... I only have to sit this out until the storm passes.'*

- Don't rise to baits. Ignore obvious put-downs and wild criticisms and unfair questions. (You can deal assertively with them later when you are both calm.) Instead, just respond with your variation on the following sample script for defusing anger. Repeat your defusing statements over and over again until their anger calms down or you or either of you leaves the scene.
- Take time out to defuse your feelings and reflect on what has happened. (But not for so long that the temptation to 'sweep things back under the carpet' takes hold.)
- Compose and prepare an assertive response to their outburst, which you will use at a later date (see sample script on pages 129–130). Or, if you feel very threatened and unable to cope, seek advice and the support of a person or people whom you can trust to defend you.

SAMPLE SCRIPT: DEFUSING
SOMEONE ELSE'S ANGER

'I agree there is a problem
[create shared ground]

... (but) I can see/hear that you are angry
 [show understanding]

*... (and) I feel uncomfortable/frightened/worried because
I can feel my own anger rising ...*
[share your feelings]

*I would like to discuss it later/tomorrow at three/when
we reach the service station/when my supervisor is here ...*
**[suggest time slot for further discussion when
tempers have cooled]**

*I think we would have a better chance of sorting it out
when we are both calm.'*
**[suggest possibility of a resolution – i.e. a
reward for calming down!]**

- **Think of a real or imaginary example of when someone has lost their cool with you.** Reread Step 10 and consider any possible triggers to their outburst from your own auto-pilot.

- **Compose and rehearse a script which you could use to 'come back' at them in an assertive, constructive manner when the storm has passed.** Use the example on the following page and the assertive language examples in Step 13 to help you. Remember that it is advisable to ask an objective friend or mentor to comment on what you have written.

SAMPLE SCRIPT: INITIATING THE FOLLOW-UP TO SOMEONE ELSE'S OUTBURST

'I'd like to talk about what happened yesterday. You became angry when ... so I didn't want to pursue the conversation
[brief objective summary of what happened]

... because I was feeling ...
[restatement of the feelings that you had in response to their anger]

I appreciate that you are very concerned about ...
[statement empathizing with their feelings or situation]

Could we discuss it now, or can we agree another mutually convenient time? And I am also keen to look at what happened
[statement of your need in relation to the incident]

... and what we can do to stop it happening again.'
[an optimistic and constructive statement to finish]

- **Bolster up your courage before going back to the fray.** For example, ring a friend or colleague whom you know to be courageous and assertive. Tell them the situation and just say that you are ringing for a confidence boost. They will be flattered and you will get the great 'send-off' you need and deserve!

Stage Four

staying cool – forever!

This stage is much more than just the 'icing on the cake' – it will help you to keep all the benefits you should have gained from the hard work you did in the other three stages. The first step will show you how you can safely and constructively siphon off anger which is being triggered but which you don't choose to deal with directly. The very last step will help by ensuring that you don't let tension build up unnecessarily over minor irritations. As it is about bringing extra fun into your life, it will also serve very well as a reward. And don't you deserve a really great one after reaching the end of this strategy?!

**Don't curse the darkness,
Light a candle.**

CHINESE PROVERB

STEP 16

Channel 'surplus' anger energy into constructive causes

In Step 11 you prepared a personal 'Conscience Charter' for yourself. You also made some decisions about the issues that were bugging you on a day-to-day basis that you felt were worth your while to express your anger over. I am sure, however, that this list will have excluded many others that still trigger your frustration, irritation and your rage. These could be issues which do not immediately affect you, or ones that you feel powerless to do much about directly. Or they may be ones that you have decided have to be put on hold for a relatively long time. The feelings that any of these bring up must not be ignored. Instead they should be channelled. *

Channelling our surplus anger purposively is so much better than just letting off the pent up steam in an ad hoc way. It turns the negative feeling into positive energy. This can be used to:

- **help yourself and further your chances of achieving dreams.** (For example, campaigning for more childcare or flexi-time to help you as a working parent, highlighting the need to keep free access to libraries so you can afford to study for a qualification)
- **alleviate the problems of others.** (For example, reduce third-world poverty, draw attention to the abuse of the human rights of certain political prisoners, raise money for neglected children or animals)
- **help the world in a more general way.** (For example, curb pollution, save wildlife, promote peace through teaching non-violent negotiation skills, and so on)

Your anger can be transformed into a powerful force for good when it is used positively and thoughtfully.

Action time!

- **Think of an ongoing issue which has been making you feel frustrated or angry for some time but which you have never set aside time to address.** For example, the broken promise of the town council to install traffic lights at a dangerous crossing, the poor standards of cleanliness of the toilets at work, the lack of commitment from the rest of your family over the caring of your elderly parents.

- **Set yourself a realistic, specific long-term goal.** For example, to have the traffic lights installed within twelve months, to have consistently clean toilets within three months, to have a family rota for visiting your parents working well by next Christmas so that you can spend that holiday abroad.

- **Find someone sympathetic to support you in your 'mission' and 'cheer' you on** (but they do not need to commit to active action – just give you genuine moral support). For example: your local councillor, a small group of colleagues who

are also concerned about the toilets, your most
caring brother or sister.

- **Plan a reward or celebration to have when
  you achieve your goal.** For example, throw a
  street party for the neighbours and invite the
  press, have a night out with colleagues, invite
  the family for a pre-Christmas meal or buy
  yourself a great outfit for Christmas in the
  Caribbean!

- **Plan your first step to be taken in the next
  week.** For example, write to your councillor, put
  matter on the agenda for your next staff meeting, ring your brother/sister.

- **Note down other ideas that could be incor-
  porated in an action plan once you have a
  clearer idea of how to proceed.** For example,
  contact press and police, contact other depart-
  ments to see if they have the same problem and
  research new cleaning company, ask friends how
  they manage or contact Age Concern for advice.

STEP 17

Give yourself an extra dose of fun

I n real life anger is rarely much fun. In fact, it might be fair to say it is almost always quite the opposite.

But ironically it is, of course, one of the richest sources of humour. Where would comedians, cartoonists and TV writers be without it? Can you imagine some of the funniest TV shows, plays and films deprived of frustrating situations and horrendous behaviour? What would *Fawlty Towers* have been like without the pomposity of Basil or *Twelfth Night* without the meanness of Malvolio? And perhaps some of you will recall how many laughs *Bridget Jones's Diary* raised from some classic frustrations in our family and love lives. Others may remember *One Flew Over the Cuckoo's Nest* which illustrated how much comedy can be drawn from the kind of dehumanizing mental health care that kept me fuming for many years.

My guess is that you would probably agree that **the world would be a much more miserable place if we humans hadn't at one stage of our evolution stumbled across our ability to laugh off at least some of our frustrations.** But how much humour is there around in your life right now?

It may be no coincidence that 'rage' appears to be becoming much more evident and unmanageable, while at the same time so many of my clients are now responding to my queries about the fun side of their life with this kind of reply:

'What fun? I've forgotten what that is ... I can't remember the last time I had a great laugh ... Nobody's finding work very funny at the moment, and life is too tense and fraught at home for much fooling around there either.'

Laughter therapy is not just good for depressives, it is good for 'blood-boilers' too. So why not bring more laughter into your life and see what a difference a small dose of daily fun can make?

Fun is one of the essential 'vitamins' you need for mental health. The more stressed you are, the more fun you need.

**The human race has only one
really effective weapon
and that is laughter.**

MARK TWAIN

Action time!

- Consult your diary (yet again!) and plan a visit to a funny play or film or comedy show *at least* once in the next month. (If you can't get out, how about a video or two?)

- Increase the amount of time you spend watching or listening to comedy shows on TV or the radio.

- Treat yourself to some comic or joke books and keep them somewhere handy so you can dip into them from time to time.

- Make a vow to spend more time with the friends who make you laugh or who you make laugh.

- If you have children, allow extra time (and give yourself more permission!) to fool around with them.

- Make a special effort over the next few weeks to think of what your favourite comedian might have made of the situation triggering your irritation.

A final word

I hope you are beginning to reap the benefits of keeping your cool. I also hope that others are too – and that they are showing their appreciation of your efforts! If they are not, ask for it! More exchange of well-deserved praise would make this a much less angry world, wouldn't it?

Don't forget that you will need to keep your Anger Guide (remember Step 3?) on everlasting duty. Some of your more deeply programmed old-anger responses could still emerge whenever you are under stress. I would also suggest that you don't rush to file this book away quite yet. Why not keep it in a handy place for the next six to twelve months. You might want to dip into it from time to time for extra encouragement and revision during times of pressure. You might also find that some of your nearest and dearest could also learn the odd thing or two from picking it up occasionally. In intimate relationships, in particular, problems with anger are rarely the sole responsibility of just one person. So, if you have done your very best and significantly improved your act, then maybe it is now time to give some others a very gentle nudge. (But remember – no sermons!)

Enjoy being cool!

Further help

Recommended reading

Maria Arapakis, *Softpower: How to Speak Up, Set Limits, and Say No without Losing Your Lover, Your Job or Your Friends* (Warner Books, 1990)

John Cook, *The Book of Positive Quotations* (Fairview Press, 1993)

Albert Ellis, *Anger: How to Live With It and Without It* (Citadel Press, 1985)

Harriet Goldhor Lerner, *The Dance of Anger* (Thorsons, 1990)

Daniel Goleman, *Working with Emotional Intelligence* (Bloomsbury,1999)

Genie Z. Laborde, *Influencing with Integrity* (Crown House Publishing, 1984)

Gael Lindenfield, *Assert Yourself* (Thorsons, 1986)

___, *Super Confidence* (Thorsons, 1989)

___, *The Positive Woman* (Thorsons, 1992)

___, *Managing Anger* (Thorsons, 1993)

___, *Self Esteem* (Thorsons, 1995)

___, *Self Motivation* (Thorsons, 1996)

___, *Emotional Confidence* (Thorsons, 1997)

___, *Success from Setbacks* (Thorsons, 1999)

___, *Confident Children* (Thorsons, 2000)

___, with Malcolm Vandenburg, *Positive Under Pressure* (Thorsons, 2000)

___, *Confident Teens* (Thorsons, 2001)

___, *Shortcuts to Bouncing Back from Heartbreak* (Thorsons, 2001)

___, *Shortcuts to Getting a Life* (Thorsons, 2001)

___, *Shortcuts to Making Hard Choices Easy* (Thorsons, 2001)

___, *Shortcuts to Believing You Can Do It* (Thorsons, 2002)

___, *Shortcuts to Finding Your Get Up and Go* (Thorsons, 2002)

Mathew McKay, Peter Rogers, Judith McKay, *When Anger Hurts: Quieting the Storm Within* (New Harbinger Publications, 1989)

Dr P. D. Sharma, *Immortal Quotations and Proverbs* (Naveet Publications, 1999)

Anthony Storr, *Human Aggression: Management Skills for Communication and Negotiation* (Penguin,1968)

Paul Wilson, *Instant Calm* (Penguin, 1995)

Cassettes

Self Motivation (Thorsons, 1997)
Self Esteem (Thorsons, 1998)
Success from Setbacks (Thorsons, 1999)
Managing Emotions at Work (Thorsons, 1999)
Emotional Confidence (Thorsons, 2000)

Available at all good bookshops, or direct from
Thorsons (0870 900 2050 or 0141 306 3349).

About the author

Contact Gael Lindenfield through her publishers:

Gael Lindenfield c/o Thorsons
HarperCollins*Publishers*
77–85 Fulham Palace Road
Hammersmith
London W6 8JB
United Kingdom

Or email: lindenfield.office@btinternet.com

For information about Gael and her current programme, visit: www.gael-lindenfield.com